CATHOLIC PLANNER
2021

_____

WELCOME

Welcome to the Catholic Planner Family! The Catholic Planner was created to help you accomplish all of your goals, stay organized, make time for yourself and your loved ones, and stay grounded in your faith throughout the year. We pray that this simple and effective tool will help you on your spiritual journey.

WHAT'S INSIDE?

Path to Sainthood: This beginning-of-the-year exercise is meant to help you reflect on the person that God is calling you to be. You will fill out each section of this chart to pinpoint your goals for 2021, while ensuring that these goals align with God's will.

Monthly Calendar: These pages give you an overview of your whole month. You will find the liturgical calendar, along with saint feast days and a saint of the month here.

There is also space to brainstorm your goals for the month. This is a great way for you to kickstart your month and move forward with focus.

Weekly Retreat: Prepare spiritually for your week here. The readings for the upcoming Sunday's mass are provided for you and a snippet of the Gospel reading is featured. We encourage you to take out your bible to read all of the passages. Below the readings you are given space to reflect on the message you read.

The next section gives you space to write down how you were in awe of God throughout the week. This allows you to always be aware of God's presence in your life and highlight what you are grateful for.

The rituals and habits section helps you to get your life into a rhythm. You can list the rituals and habits you want to develop and check off the days you accomplish each one. Good daily habits are personal activities that are important to your own well-being (i.e. drinking 8 glasses of water, exercising, practicing a passion, etc.). Catholic rituals are religious activities that express your love for Christ (i.e. attending daily mass, attending a scripture study, performing acts of charity, etc.).

The prayer list helps you to add focus and structure to your communion with God.

Weekly Calendar: These pages give you space for you to schedule your daily appointments and jot down any notes and tasks to do throughout the week.

MAKE IT YOUR OWN

There are many ways to use the Catholic Planner. Discover the best way to use the Catholic Planner that is most effective for you. Put your personality into it and add some color. Make it your own!

KEEP IN TOUCH

For more tips on how to use the Catholic Planner visit us at CatholicPlanner.com. Follow us on Facebook at Facebook.com/CatholicPlanner and on Instagram and Twitter @CatholicPlanner. Share how you've personalized your Catholic Planner and tag us!

PATH TO SAINTHOOD GUIDE

Make this your best year ever by setting goals for yourself for 2021! The Path to Sainthood helps you to look deep into what God's purpose is for you, so that you can come up with these goals.

> "Jesus, help me to simplify my life by learning what You want me to be and becoming that person."
> - Saint Therese of Lisieux -

INSTRUCTIONS

2020 Achievements: Write down the achievements you were most proud of accomplishing last year - big or small.

God's Blessings: Reflect on the gifts that God has brought into your life. What are you most grateful for? What talents and curiosities has he given you?

Inspiration: Write down the names of people who are inspirations in your life. These can be saints, friends, family, priests, teachers, or anyone else you can think of. Also write down the qualities and traits that make these people inspirations to you.

Focus: Reflect on the categories in your life that you feel called to focus on, develop, work on, or maintain. Examples of these categories can be the Seven Virtues, the Fruit of the Spirit (Galatians 5:22-23), your family, your career, or your creativity.

2021 Goals: After filling out the previous sections you should have a better idea of what is most important to you and what God is calling you to do or be. Set goals for yourself based on the direction given to you from your answers. Don't be afraid to dream big!

> "Be who God meant you to be and you will set the world on fire."
> - Saint Catherine of Siena -

MY PATH TO SAINTHOOD

2020 ACHIEVEMENTS

GOD'S BLESSINGS

2021 GOALS

INSPIRATION

FOCUS

PATH TO SAINTHOOD

Use this space for brainstorming.

PATH TO SAINTHOOD

Use this space for brainstorming.

40 DAY LENTEN CHALLENGE

I WILL PREPARE FOR CHRIST'S DEATH & RESURRECTION BY

Brainstorm and choose what you feel called to commit to during the Lenten Season.

REFLECT

Why did you choose to commit to this?

MY SUPPORT TEAM

Who can help you along the way?

1	2	3	4	5	6	7	8	9	10	11	12	13	14	15	16	17	18	19	20
21	22	23	24	25	26	27	28	29	30	31	32	33	34	35	36	37	38	39	40

Initial after you complete each day.

2021

JANUARY

S	M	T	W	T	F	S
					1	2
3	4	5	6	7	8	9
10	11	12	13	14	15	16
17	18	19	20	21	22	23
24	25	26	27	28	29	30
31						

FEBRUARY

S	M	T	W	T	F	S
	1	2	3	4	5	6
7	8	9	10	11	12	13
14	15	16	17	18	19	20
21	22	23	24	25	26	27
28						

MARCH

S	M	T	W	T	F	S
	1	2	3	4	5	6
7	8	9	10	11	12	13
14	15	16	17	18	19	20
21	22	23	24	25	26	27
28	29	30	31			

APRIL

S	M	T	W	T	F	S
				1	2	3
4	5	6	7	8	9	10
11	12	13	14	15	16	17
18	19	20	21	22	23	24
25	26	27	28	29	30	

MAY

S	M	T	W	T	F	S
						1
2	3	4	5	6	7	8
9	10	11	12	13	14	15
16	17	18	19	20	21	22
23	24	25	26	27	28	29
30	31					

JUNE

S	M	T	W	T	F	S
		1	2	3	4	5
6	7	8	9	10	11	12
13	14	15	16	17	18	19
20	21	22	23	24	25	26
27	28	29	30			

JULY

S	M	T	W	T	F	S
				1	2	3
4	5	6	7	8	9	10
11	12	13	14	15	16	17
18	19	20	21	22	23	24
25	26	27	28	29	30	31

AUGUST

S	M	T	W	T	F	S
1	2	3	4	5	6	7
8	9	10	11	12	13	14
15	16	17	18	19	20	21
22	23	24	25	26	27	28
29	30	31				

SEPTEMBER

S	M	T	W	T	F	S
			1	2	3	4
5	6	7	8	9	10	11
12	13	14	15	16	17	18
19	20	21	22	23	24	25
26	27	28	29	30		

OCTOBER

S	M	T	W	T	F	S
					1	2
3	4	5	6	7	8	9
10	11	12	13	14	15	16
17	18	19	20	21	22	23
24	25	26	27	28	29	30
31						

NOVEMBER

S	M	T	W	T	F	S
	1	2	3	4	5	6
7	8	9	10	11	12	13
14	15	16	17	18	19	20
21	22	23	24	25	26	27
28	29	30				

DECEMBER

S	M	T	W	T	F	S
			1	2	3	4
5	6	7	8	9	10	11
12	13	14	15	16	17	18
19	20	21	22	23	24	25
26	27	28	29	30	31	

JANUARY	SUNDAY	MONDAY	TUESDAY
NOTES			
	3 — The Epiphany of the Lord	4 — *Saint Elizabeth Ann Seton*	5 — *Saint John Neumann*
	10 — The Baptism of the Lord	11	12
	17 — Second Sunday in Ordinary Time	18 — *Martin Luther King, Jr. Day*	19
	24 — Third Sunday in Ordinary Time	25 — The Conversion of Saint Paul the Apostle	26
	31 — Fourth Sunday in Ordinary Time		

SAINT SEBASTIAN

- Feast Day: January 20
- Born: 256; Died: 288
- Patron saint of soldiers and athletes
- He served in the Roman army to assist other Christians being persecuted by the Romans.
- He was promoted to the Praetorian Guard to protect Emperor Diocletian.
- Twin deacons were arrested for refusing to make public sacrifices. Their parents tried to persuade them to renounce Christianity. Sebastian then converted the parents.
- Sebastian was ordered to be killed by being tied to a post and shot with arrows, but survived.
- He warned Diocletian of his sins and was killed.

WEDNESDAY	THURSDAY	FRIDAY	SATURDAY
		1 **Solemnity of Mary, the Holy Mother of God** *New Year's Day*	2 Saints Basil the Great & Gregory Nazianzen
6 Saint André Bessette	7 Saint Raymond of Penyafort	8	9
13 Saint Hilary	14	15	16
20 Saint Fabian Saint Sebastian	21 Saint Agnes	22 Day of Prayer for the Legal Protection of Unborn Children	23 Saint Vincent Saint Marianne Cope
27 Saint Angela Merici	28 Saint Thomas Aquinas	29	30

GOALS

WEEKLY RETREAT • DECEMBER 27, 2020

READING 1	READING 2	GOSPEL
Sirach 3:2-6, 12-14	Colossians 3:12-21	Luke 2:22-40

Now there was a man in Jerusalem whose name was Simeon. This man was righteous and devout, awaiting the consolation of Israel, and the holy Spirit was upon him. It had been revealed to him by the holy Spirit that he should not see death before he had seen the Messiah of the Lord.

Luke 2:25-26

REFLECTION

HOW WERE YOU IN AWE OF GOD THIS WEEK?

WEEKLY RETREAT

FREE SPACE

HABITS & RITUALS

S	M	T	W	T	F	S
S	M	T	W	T	F	S
S	M	T	W	T	F	S
S	M	T	W	T	F	S
S	M	T	W	T	F	S

PRAYER LIST

DEC & JAN	SUNDAY 27	MONDAY 28	TUESDAY 29
PRIORITIES	MORNING	MORNING	MORNING
	DAY	DAY	DAY
	NIGHT	NIGHT	NIGHT

NOTES

WEDNESDAY 30	THURSDAY 31	FRIDAY 1	SATURDAY 2
MORNING	MORNING	**Solemnity of Mary** *New Year's Day* MORNING	MORNING
DAY	DAY	DAY	DAY
NIGHT	NIGHT	NIGHT	NIGHT

TO DO LIST

- [ ]
- [ ]
- [ ]
- [ ]
- [ ]
- [ ]
- [ ]
- [ ]
- [ ]
- [ ]

- [ ]
- [ ]
- [ ]
- [ ]
- [ ]
- [ ]
- [ ]
- [ ]
- [ ]
- [ ]

WEEKLY RETREAT • JANUARY 3, 2021

READING 1	READING 2	GOSPEL
Isaiah 60:1-6	Ephesians 3:2-3a, 5-6	Matthew 2:1-12

They were overjoyed at seeing the star, and on entering the house they saw the child with Mary his mother. They prostrated themselves and did him homage. Then they opened their treasures and offered him gifts of gold, frankincense, and myrrh.

Matthew 2:10-11

REFLECTION

HOW WERE YOU IN AWE OF GOD THIS WEEK?

WEEKLY RETREAT

FREE SPACE

HABITS & RITUALS							PRAYER LIST
S	M	T	W	T	F	S	
S	M	T	W	T	F	S	
S	M	T	W	T	F	S	
S	M	T	W	T	F	S	
S	M	T	W	T	F	S	

JANUARY	SUNDAY 3	MONDAY 4	TUESDAY 5
PRIORITIES	The Epiphany of the Lord	MORNING	MORNING
	DAY	DAY	DAY
	NIGHT	NIGHT	NIGHT

NOTES

WEDNESDAY 6	THURSDAY 7	FRIDAY 8	SATURDAY 9
MORNING	MORNING	MORNING	MORNING
DAY	DAY	DAY	DAY
NIGHT	NIGHT	NIGHT	NIGHT

TO DO LIST

WEEKLY RETREAT • JANUARY 10, 2021

READING 1	READING 2	GOSPEL
Isaiah 42:1-4, 6-7	Acts 10:34-38	Mark 1:7-11

It happened in those days that Jesus came from Nazareth of Galilee and was baptized in the Jordan by John. On coming up out of the water he saw the heavens being torn open and the Spirit, like a dove, descending upon him. And a voice came from the heavens, "You are my beloved Son; with you I am well pleased."

Mark 1:9-11

REFLECTION

HOW WERE YOU IN AWE OF GOD THIS WEEK?

WEEKLY RETREAT

FREE SPACE

HABITS & RITUALS

S	M	T	W	T	F	S
S	M	T	W	T	F	S
S	M	T	W	T	F	S
S	M	T	W	T	F	S
S	M	T	W	T	F	S

PRAYER LIST

JANUARY	SUNDAY	MONDAY	TUESDAY
PRIORITIES	10	11	12
	The Baptism of the Lord	MORNING	MORNING
	DAY	DAY	DAY
	NIGHT	NIGHT	NIGHT

NOTES

WEDNESDAY 13	THURSDAY 14	FRIDAY 15	SATURDAY 16
MORNING	MORNING	MORNING	MORNING
DAY	DAY	DAY	DAY
NIGHT	NIGHT	NIGHT	NIGHT

TO DO LIST

WEEKLY RETREAT • JANUARY 17, 2021

READING 1	READING 2	GOSPEL
1 Samuel 3:3b-10, 19	1 Cor 6:13c-15a, 17-20	John 1:35-42

The next day John was there again with two of his disciples, and as he watched Jesus walk by, he said, "Behold, the Lamb of God." The two disciples heard what he said and followed Jesus.

John 1:35-37

REFLECTION

HOW WERE YOU IN AWE OF GOD THIS WEEK?

WEEKLY RETREAT

FREE SPACE

HABITS & RITUALS

| S | M | T | W | T | F | S |

| S | M | T | W | T | F | S |

| S | M | T | W | T | F | S |

| S | M | T | W | T | F | S |

| S | M | T | W | T | F | S |

PRAYER LIST

_____
_____
_____
_____
_____
_____
_____
_____
_____
_____

JANUARY	SUNDAY 17	MONDAY 18	TUESDAY 19
PRIORITIES	MORNING	*Martin Luther King, Jr. Day*	MORNING
	DAY	DAY	DAY
	NIGHT	NIGHT	NIGHT

NOTES

WEDNESDAY 20	THURSDAY 21	FRIDAY 22	SATURDAY 23
MORNING	MORNING	MORNING	MORNING
DAY	DAY	DAY	DAY
NIGHT	NIGHT	NIGHT	NIGHT

TO DO LIST

WEEKLY RETREAT • JANUARY 24, 2021

READING 1	READING 2	GOSPEL
Jonah 3:1-5, 10	1 Corinthians 7:29-31	Mark 1:14-20

After John had been arrested, Jesus came to Galilee proclaiming the gospel of God: "This is the time of fulfillment. The kingdom of God is at hand. Repent, and believe in the gospel."

Mark 1:14-15

REFLECTION

HOW WERE YOU IN AWE OF GOD THIS WEEK?

WEEKLY RETREAT

FREE SPACE

HABITS & RITUALS

| S | M | T | W | T | F | S |

| S | M | T | W | T | F | S |

| S | M | T | W | T | F | S |

| S | M | T | W | T | F | S |

| S | M | T | W | T | F | S |

PRAYER LIST

JANUARY	SUNDAY 24	MONDAY 25	TUESDAY 26
PRIORITIES	MORNING	MORNING	MORNING
	DAY	DAY	DAY
	NIGHT	NIGHT	NIGHT

NOTES

WEDNESDAY 27	THURSDAY 28	FRIDAY 29	SATURDAY 30
MORNING	MORNING	MORNING	MORNING
DAY	DAY	DAY	DAY
NIGHT	NIGHT	NIGHT	NIGHT

TO DO LIST

- [ ] _____
- [ ] _____
- [ ] _____
- [ ] _____
- [ ] _____
- [ ] _____
- [ ] _____
- [ ] _____
- [ ] _____
- [ ] _____

- [ ] _____
- [ ] _____
- [ ] _____
- [ ] _____
- [ ] _____
- [ ] _____
- [ ] _____
- [ ] _____
- [ ] _____
- [ ] _____

FEBRUARY	SUNDAY	MONDAY	TUESDAY
NOTES		1	2 The Presentation of the Lord
	7 Fifth Sunday in Ordinary Time	8 Saint Jerome Emiliani / Saint Josephine Bakhita	9
	14 Sixth Sunday in Ordinary Time / Valentine's Day	15 *President's Day*	16
	21 First Sunday of Lent	22 The Chair of Saint Peter the Apostle	23 Saint Polycarp
	28 Second Sunday of Lent		

SAINT DOROTHY

- Feast Day: February 6
- Born: c.279–290; Died: c.311
- Patron saint of brewers, brides, florists, gardeners, and newlyweds
- She suffered persecution under Emperor Diocletian and was tortured and sentenced to death.
- On her way to execution, a pagan lawyer mocked her by telling her to send fruits from Christ's garden that she would soon be in.
- She sent her headdress to him before her execution, which was found filled with fruits and roses.
- The pagan lawyer, Theophilus, then converted.

WEDNESDAY	THURSDAY	FRIDAY	SATURDAY
3 Saint Blaise Saint Ansgar	4	5 Saint Agatha	6 Saint Paul Miki & Companions Saint Dorothy
10 Saint Scholastica	11 Our Lady of Lourdes	12	13
17 Ash Wednesday	18	19	20
24	25	26	27

GOALS

WEEKLY RETREAT • JANUARY 31, 2021

READING 1	READING 2	GOSPEL
Deuteronomy 18:15-20	1 Corinthians 7:32-35	Mark 1:21-28

The unclean spirit convulsed him and with a loud cry came out of him. All were amazed and asked one another, "What is this? A new teaching with authority. He commands even the unclean spirits and they obey him." His fame spread everywhere throughout the whole region of Galilee.

Mark 1:26-28

REFLECTION

HOW WERE YOU IN AWE OF GOD THIS WEEK?

WEEKLY RETREAT

FREE SPACE

HABITS & RITUALS

S	M	T	W	T	F	S
S	M	T	W	T	F	S
S	M	T	W	T	F	S
S	M	T	W	T	F	S
S	M	T	W	T	F	S

PRAYER LIST

JAN & FEB	SUNDAY 31	MONDAY 1	TUESDAY 2
PRIORITIES	MORNING	MORNING	MORNING
	DAY	DAY	DAY
	NIGHT	NIGHT	NIGHT

NOTES

WEDNESDAY 3	THURSDAY 4	FRIDAY 5	SATURDAY 6
MORNING	MORNING	MORNING	MORNING
DAY	DAY	DAY	DAY
NIGHT	NIGHT	NIGHT	NIGHT

TO DO LIST

☐ _____ ☐ _____
☐ _____ ☐ _____
☐ _____ ☐ _____
☐ _____ ☐ _____
☐ _____ ☐ _____
☐ _____ ☐ _____
☐ _____ ☐ _____
☐ _____ ☐ _____
☐ _____ ☐ _____
☐ _____ ☐ _____

WEEKLY RETREAT • FEBRUARY 7, 2021

READING 1	READING 2	GOSPEL
Job 7:1-4, 6-7	1 Cor 9:16-19, 22-23	Mark 1:29-39

He told them, "Let us go on to the nearby villages that I may preach there also. For this purpose have I come." So he went into their synagogues, preaching and driving out demons throughout the whole of Galilee.

Mark 1:38-39

REFLECTION

HOW WERE YOU IN AWE OF GOD THIS WEEK?

WEEKLY RETREAT

FREE SPACE

HABITS & RITUALS

S	M	T	W	T	F	S
S	M	T	W	T	F	S
S	M	T	W	T	F	S
S	M	T	W	T	F	S
S	M	T	W	T	F	S

PRAYER LIST

FEBRUARY	SUNDAY 7	MONDAY 8	TUESDAY 9
PRIORITIES	MORNING	MORNING	MORNING
	DAY	DAY	DAY
	NIGHT	NIGHT	NIGHT

NOTES

WEDNESDAY 10	THURSDAY 11	FRIDAY 12	SATURDAY 13
MORNING	MORNING	MORNING	MORNING
DAY	DAY	DAY	DAY
NIGHT	NIGHT	NIGHT	NIGHT

TO DO LIST

WEEKLY RETREAT • FEBRUARY 14, 2021

READING 1	READING 2	GOSPEL
Leviticus 13:1-2, 44-46	1 Corinthians 10:31—11:1	Mark 1:40-45

The man went away and began to publicize the whole matter. He spread the report abroad so that it was impossible for Jesus to enter a town openly. He remained outside in deserted places, and people kept coming to him from everywhere.

Mark 1:45

REFLECTION

___

HOW WERE YOU IN AWE OF GOD THIS WEEK?

WEEKLY RETREAT

FREE SPACE

HABITS & RITUALS

S	M	T	W	T	F	S
S	M	T	W	T	F	S
S	M	T	W	T	F	S
S	M	T	W	T	F	S
S	M	T	W	T	F	S

PRAYER LIST

FEBRUARY	SUNDAY 14	MONDAY 15	TUESDAY 16
PRIORITIES	*Valentine's Day*	*President's Day*	MORNING
	DAY	DAY	DAY
	NIGHT	NIGHT	NIGHT

NOTES

WEDNESDAY 17	THURSDAY 18	FRIDAY 19	SATURDAY 20
Ash Wednesday	MORNING	MORNING	MORNING
DAY	DAY	DAY	DAY
NIGHT	NIGHT	NIGHT	NIGHT

TO DO LIST

WEEKLY RETREAT • FEBRUARY 21, 2021

READING 1	READING 2	GOSPEL
Genesis 9:8-15	1 Peter 3:18-22	Mark 1:12-15

At once the Spirit drove him out into the desert, and he remained in the desert for forty days, tempted by Satan. He was among wild beasts, and the angels ministered to him.

Mark 1:12-13

REFLECTION

HOW WERE YOU IN AWE OF GOD THIS WEEK?

WEEKLY RETREAT

FREE SPACE

HABITS & RITUALS

S	M	T	W	T	F	S
S	M	T	W	T	F	S
S	M	T	W	T	F	S
S	M	T	W	T	F	S
S	M	T	W	T	F	S

PRAYER LIST

FEBRUARY	SUNDAY 21	MONDAY 22	TUESDAY 23
PRIORITIES	MORNING	MORNING	MORNING
	DAY	DAY	DAY
	NIGHT	NIGHT	NIGHT

NOTES

WEDNESDAY 24	THURSDAY 25	FRIDAY 26	SATURDAY 27
MORNING	MORNING	MORNING	MORNING
DAY	DAY	DAY	DAY
NIGHT	NIGHT	NIGHT	NIGHT

TO DO LIST

MARCH	SUNDAY	MONDAY	TUESDAY
NOTES		1	2
	7 Third Sunday of Lent	8 Saint John of God	9 Saint Frances of Rome
	14 Fourth Sunday of Lent *Daylight Saving Time*	15	16
	21 Fifth Sunday of Lent Saint Nicholas of Flüe	22	23 Saint Turibius of Mogrovejo
	28 Palm Sunday of the Passion of the Lord	29	30

SAINT NICHOLAS OF FLÜE

- Feast Day: March 21
- Born: c.1417-1421; Died: March 1487
- Patron saint of Switzerland
- He was a military leader who fought with a sword in one hard and a rosary in the other.
- After receiving a mystical vision of a lily eaten by a horse, he took up the life of a hermit.
- He is said to have survived for nineteen years with no food except for the Holy Eucharist.
- He was visited by those who sought spiritual council throughout Europe.
- His intervention in a conflict over the admission of Fribourg and Solothurn to the Swiss Confederation helped prevent civil war.

WEDNESDAY	THURSDAY	FRIDAY	SATURDAY
3 Saint Katharine Drexel	4 Saint Casimir	5	6
10	11	12	13
17 Saint Patrick	18 Saint Cyril of Jerusalem	19 Saint Joseph, Spouse of the Blessed Virgin Mary	20
24	25 The Annunciation of the Lord	26	27
31			

GOALS

WEEKLY RETREAT • FEBRUARY 28, 2021

READING 1	READING 2	GOSPEL
Gen 22:1-2, 9a, 10-13, 15-18	Romans 8:31b-34	Mark 9:2-10

After six days Jesus took Peter, James, and John and led them up a high mountain apart by themselves. And he was transfigured before them, and his clothes became dazzling white, such as no fuller on earth could bleach them.

Mark 9:2-3

REFLECTION

HOW WERE YOU IN AWE OF GOD THIS WEEK?

WEEKLY RETREAT

FREE SPACE

HABITS & RITUALS	PRAYER LIST

S	M	T	W	T	F	S

S	M	T	W	T	F	S

S	M	T	W	T	F	S

S	M	T	W	T	F	S

S	M	T	W	T	F	S

FEB & MAR	SUNDAY 28	MONDAY 1	TUESDAY 2
PRIORITIES	MORNING	MORNING	MORNING
	DAY	DAY	DAY
	NIGHT	NIGHT	NIGHT

NOTES

WEDNESDAY 3	THURSDAY 4	FRIDAY 5	SATURDAY 6
MORNING	MORNING	MORNING	MORNING
DAY	DAY	DAY	DAY
NIGHT	NIGHT	NIGHT	NIGHT

TO DO LIST

- [ ] _____
- [ ] _____
- [ ] _____
- [ ] _____
- [ ] _____
- [ ] _____
- [ ] _____
- [ ] _____
- [ ] _____
- [ ] _____

- [ ] _____
- [ ] _____
- [ ] _____
- [ ] _____
- [ ] _____
- [ ] _____
- [ ] _____
- [ ] _____
- [ ] _____
- [ ] _____

WEEKLY RETREAT • MARCH 7, 2021

READING 1	READING 2	GOSPEL
Exodus 20:1-17	1 Corinthians 1:22-25	John 2:13-25

Jesus answered and said to them, "Destroy this temple and in three days I will raise it up." The Jews said, "This temple has been under construction for forty-six years, and you will raise it up in three days?" But he was speaking about the temple of his body.

John 2:19-21

REFLECTION

HOW WERE YOU IN AWE OF GOD THIS WEEK?

WEEKLY RETREAT

FREE SPACE

HABITS & RITUALS							PRAYER LIST
S	M	T	W	T	F	S	
S	M	T	W	T	F	S	
S	M	T	W	T	F	S	
S	M	T	W	T	F	S	
S	M	T	W	T	F	S	

MARCH	SUNDAY 7	MONDAY 8	TUESDAY 9
PRIORITIES	MORNING	MORNING	MORNING
	DAY	DAY	DAY
	NIGHT	NIGHT	NIGHT

NOTES

WEDNESDAY 10	THURSDAY 11	FRIDAY 12	SATURDAY 13
MORNING	MORNING	MORNING	MORNING
DAY	DAY	DAY	DAY
NIGHT	NIGHT	NIGHT	NIGHT

TO DO LIST

WEEKLY RETREAT • MARCH 14, 2021

READING 1	READING 2	GOSPEL
2 Chr 36:14-16, 19-23	Ephesians 2:4-10	John 3:14-21

For God so loved the world that he gave his only Son, so that everyone who believes in him might not perish but might have eternal life. For God did not send his Son into the world to condemn the world, but that the world might be saved through him.

John 3:16-17

REFLECTION

HOW WERE YOU IN AWE OF GOD THIS WEEK?

WEEKLY RETREAT

FREE SPACE

HABITS & RITUALS	PRAYER LIST

S	M	T	W	T	F	S
S	M	T	W	T	F	S
S	M	T	W	T	F	S
S	M	T	W	T	F	S
S	M	T	W	T	F	S

MARCH	SUNDAY 14	MONDAY 15	TUESDAY 16
PRIORITIES	*Daylight Saving Time*	MORNING	MORNING
	DAY	DAY	DAY
	NIGHT	NIGHT	NIGHT

NOTES

WEDNESDAY 17	THURSDAY 18	FRIDAY 19	SATURDAY 20
MORNING	MORNING	Saint Joseph, Spouse of the Blessed Virgin Mary	MORNING
DAY	DAY	DAY	DAY
NIGHT	NIGHT	NIGHT	NIGHT

TO DO LIST

- [ ]
- [ ]
- [ ]
- [ ]
- [ ]
- [ ]
- [ ]
- [ ]
- [ ]
- [ ]

- [ ]
- [ ]
- [ ]
- [ ]
- [ ]
- [ ]
- [ ]
- [ ]
- [ ]

WEEKLY RETREAT • MARCH 21, 2021

READING 1	READING 2	GOSPEL
Jeremiah 31:31-34	Hebrews 5:7-9	John 12:20-33

Amen, amen, I say to you, unless a grain of wheat falls to the ground and dies, it remains just a grain of wheat; but if it dies, it produces much fruit. Whoever loves his life loses it, and whoever hates his life in this world will preserve it for eternal life.

John 12:24-25

REFLECTION

HOW WERE YOU IN AWE OF GOD THIS WEEK?

WEEKLY RETREAT

FREE SPACE

HABITS & RITUALS

S	M	T	W	T	F	S
S	M	T	W	T	F	S
S	M	T	W	T	F	S
S	M	T	W	T	F	S
S	M	T	W	T	F	S

PRAYER LIST

MARCH	SUNDAY 21	MONDAY 22	TUESDAY 23
PRIORITIES	MORNING	MORNING	MORNING
	DAY	DAY	DAY
	NIGHT	NIGHT	NIGHT

NOTES

WEDNESDAY 24	THURSDAY 25	FRIDAY 26	SATURDAY 27
MORNING	The Annunciation of the Lord	MORNING	MORNING
DAY	DAY	DAY	DAY
NIGHT	NIGHT	NIGHT	NIGHT

TO DO LIST

APRIL	SUNDAY	MONDAY	TUESDAY
NOTES			
	4 Easter Sunday	5	6
	11 Second Sunday of Easter (Sunday of Divine Mercy) — Saint Gemma Galgani	12	13 — Saint Martin I
	18 Third Sunday of Easter	19	20
	25 Fourth Sunday of Easter	26	27

SAINT GEMMA GALGANI

- Feast Day: April 11
- Born: 1878; Died: April 11, 1903
- Patron saint of students, pharmacists, against temptation, and against loss of parents
- She was known as the "Flower of Lucca."
- She attended a Catholic boarding school and developed a love for prayer at a young age.
- She developed spinal meningitis at the age of 16 and prayed to the Sacred Heart of Jesus.
- At the age of 16, she became the mother figure to her younger siblings when her father died.
- She experienced stigmata at the age of 21.
- She often saw and spoke to her guardian angel, Jesus, Mary, and other saints.

WEDNESDAY	THURSDAY	FRIDAY	SATURDAY
	1 Holy Thursday	2 Good Friday Saint Francis of Paola	3 Holy Saturday
7 Saint John Baptist de la Salle	8	9	10
14	15 Tax Day	16 Saint Bernadette	17
21 Saint Anselm	22 Earth Day	23 Saint George Saint Adalbert	24 Saint Fidelis of Sigmaringen
28 Saint Peter Chanel Saint Louis Grignion de Montfort	29 Saint Catherine of Siena	30 Saint Pius V	

GOALS

WEEKLY RETREAT • MARCH 28, 2021

READING 1	READING 2	GOSPEL
Isaiah 50:4-7	Philippians 2:6-11	Mark 14:1—15:47

Then Judas Iscariot, one of the Twelve, went off to the chief priests to hand him over to them. When they heard him they were pleased and promised to pay him money. Then he looked for an opportunity to hand him over.

Mark 14:10-11

REFLECTION

HOW WERE YOU IN AWE OF GOD THIS WEEK?

WEEKLY RETREAT

FREE SPACE

HABITS & RITUALS

S	M	T	W	T	F	S
S	M	T	W	T	F	S
S	M	T	W	T	F	S
S	M	T	W	T	F	S
S	M	T	W	T	F	S

PRAYER LIST

| MAR & APR | SUNDAY 28 | MONDAY 29 | TUESDAY 30 |

PRIORITIES

SUNDAY 28
Palm Sunday

MORNING

DAY

NIGHT

MONDAY 29
MORNING

DAY

NIGHT

TUESDAY 30
MORNING

DAY

NIGHT

NOTES

WEDNESDAY	THURSDAY	FRIDAY	SATURDAY
31	1	2	3
MORNING	Holy Thursday	Good Friday	Holy Saturday
DAY	DAY	DAY	DAY
NIGHT	NIGHT	NIGHT	NIGHT

TO DO LIST

- [ ] _____
- [ ] _____
- [ ] _____
- [ ] _____
- [ ] _____
- [ ] _____
- [ ] _____
- [ ] _____
- [ ] _____
- [ ] _____

- [ ] _____
- [ ] _____
- [ ] _____
- [ ] _____
- [ ] _____
- [ ] _____
- [ ] _____
- [ ] _____
- [ ] _____
- [ ] _____

WEEKLY RETREAT • APRIL 4, 2021

READING 1	READING 2	GOSPEL
Acts 10:34a, 37-43	Colossians 3:1-4	John 20:1-9

When Simon Peter arrived after him, he went into the tomb and saw the burial cloths there, and the cloth that had covered his head, not with the burial cloths but rolled up in a separate place. Then the other disciple also went in, the one who had arrived at the tomb first, and he saw and believed.

John 20:6-8

REFLECTION

HOW WERE YOU IN AWE OF GOD THIS WEEK?

WEEKLY RETREAT

FREE SPACE

HABITS & RITUALS

S	M	T	W	T	F	S
S	M	T	W	T	F	S
S	M	T	W	T	F	S
S	M	T	W	T	F	S
S	M	T	W	T	F	S

PRAYER LIST

APRIL	SUNDAY 4	MONDAY 5	TUESDAY 6
PRIORITIES	Easter Sunday	MORNING	MORNING
	DAY	DAY	DAY
	NIGHT	NIGHT	NIGHT

NOTES

WEDNESDAY 7

MORNING

DAY

NIGHT

THURSDAY 8

MORNING

DAY

NIGHT

FRIDAY 9

MORNING

DAY

NIGHT

SATURDAY 10

MORNING

DAY

NIGHT

TO DO LIST

- [ ]
- [ ]
- [ ]
- [ ]
- [ ]
- [ ]
- [ ]
- [ ]
- [ ]
- [ ]

- [ ]
- [ ]
- [ ]
- [ ]
- [ ]
- [ ]
- [ ]
- [ ]
- [ ]
- [ ]

WEEKLY RETREAT • APRIL 11, 2021

READING 1	READING 2	GOSPEL
Acts 4:32-35	1 John 5:1-6	John 20:19-31

Thomas, called Didymus, one of the Twelve, was not with them when Jesus came. So the other disciples said to him, "We have seen the Lord." But he said to them, "Unless I see the mark of the nails in his hands and put my finger into the nailmarks and put my hand into his side, I will not believe."

John 20:24-25

REFLECTION

HOW WERE YOU IN AWE OF GOD THIS WEEK?

WEEKLY RETREAT

FREE SPACE

HABITS & RITUALS

| S | M | T | W | T | F | S |

| S | M | T | W | T | F | S |

| S | M | T | W | T | F | S |

| S | M | T | W | T | F | S |

| S | M | T | W | T | F | S |

PRAYER LIST

APRIL	SUNDAY 11	MONDAY 12	TUESDAY 13
PRIORITIES	Sunday of Divine Mercy	MORNING	MORNING
	DAY	DAY	DAY
	NIGHT	NIGHT	NIGHT

NOTES

WEDNESDAY 14	THURSDAY 15	FRIDAY 16	SATURDAY 17
MORNING	*Tax Day*	MORNING	MORNING
DAY	DAY	DAY	DAY
NIGHT	NIGHT	NIGHT	NIGHT

TO DO LIST

- ☐ _____
- ☐ _____
- ☐ _____
- ☐ _____
- ☐ _____
- ☐ _____
- ☐ _____
- ☐ _____
- ☐ _____
- ☐ _____

- ☐ _____
- ☐ _____
- ☐ _____
- ☐ _____
- ☐ _____
- ☐ _____
- ☐ _____
- ☐ _____
- ☐ _____
- ☐ _____

WEEKLY RETREAT • APRIL 18, 2021

READING 1	READING 2	GOSPEL
Acts 3:13-15, 17-19	1 John 2:1-5a	Luke 24:35-48

After three days they found him in the temple, sitting in the midst of the teachers, listening to them and asking them questions, and all who heard him were astounded at his understanding and his answers.

Luke 2:46-47

REFLECTION

_____
_____
_____
_____
_____
_____
_____
_____
_____
_____
_____
_____
_____
_____
_____
_____
_____

HOW WERE YOU IN AWE OF GOD THIS WEEK?

WEEKLY RETREAT

FREE SPACE

HABITS & RITUALS	PRAYER LIST

S M T W T F S

S M T W T F S

S M T W T F S

S M T W T F S

S M T W T F S

APRIL	SUNDAY 18	MONDAY 19	TUESDAY 20
PRIORITIES	MORNING	MORNING	MORNING
	DAY	DAY	DAY
	NIGHT	NIGHT	NIGHT

NOTES

WEDNESDAY 21	THURSDAY 22	FRIDAY 23	SATURDAY 24
MORNING	*Earth Day* MORNING	MORNING	MORNING
DAY	DAY	DAY	DAY
NIGHT	NIGHT	NIGHT	NIGHT

TO DO LIST

- [ ] _____
- [ ] _____
- [ ] _____
- [ ] _____
- [ ] _____
- [ ] _____
- [ ] _____
- [ ] _____
- [ ] _____
- [ ] _____

- [ ] _____
- [ ] _____
- [ ] _____
- [ ] _____
- [ ] _____
- [ ] _____
- [ ] _____
- [ ] _____
- [ ] _____
- [ ] _____

MAY

SUNDAY	MONDAY	TUESDAY
NOTES		
2 — Fifth Sunday of Easter	3 — Saints Philip & James	4
9 — Sixth Sunday of Easter *Mother's Day*	10 — Saint Damien de Veuster	11
16 — The Ascension of the Lord/ Seventh Sunday of Easter*	17	18 — Saint John I
23 — Pentecost Sunday	24 — The Blessed Virgin Mary, Mother of the Church *Victoria Day (CA)*	25 — Saint Bede the Venerable, Saint Gregory VII, Saint Mary Magdalene de' Pazzi
30 — The Most Holy Trinity	31 — The Visitation of the Blessed Virgin Mary *Memorial Day*	

SAINT MARY MAGDALENE DE' PAZZI

- Feast Day: May 25
- Born: April 2, 1566; Died: March 25, 1607
- Patron saint of sick people and against temptation
- She was born to one of the wealthiest noble families of Renaissance Florence.
- She took a vow of virginity at a young age.
- She experienced her first religious ecstasy at the age of 12 and continued to exhibit many mystical experiences thereafter.
- She was educated at a monastery of nuns.
- During her ecstasies, she dictated her experiences to her fellow nuns and filled five large books over six years.

WEDNESDAY	THURSDAY	FRIDAY	SATURDAY
			1 Saint Joseph the Worker
5	6	7	8
12 Saints Nereus & Achilleus Saint Pancras	13 The Ascension of the Lord*	14 Saint Matthias	15 Saint Isidore Saint Dymphna
19	20 Saint Bernadine of Siena	21 Saint Christopher Magallanes & Companions	22 Saint Rita of Cascia
26 Saint Philip Neri	27 Saint Augustine of Canterbury	28	29 Saint Paul VI

*Ecclesiastical Provinces of Boston, Hartford, New York, Newark, Omaha, Philadelphia

GOALS

WEEKLY RETREAT • APRIL 25, 2021

READING 1	READING 2	GOSPEL
Acts 4:8-12	1 John 3:1-2	John 10:11-18

I am the good shepherd. A good shepherd lays down his life for the sheep. A hired man, who is not a shepherd and whose sheep are not his own, sees a wolf coming and leaves the sheep and runs away, and the wolf catches and scatters them. This is because he works for pay and has no concern for the sheep.

John 10:11-13

REFLECTION

HOW WERE YOU IN AWE OF GOD THIS WEEK?

WEEKLY RETREAT

FREE SPACE

HABITS & RITUALS

| S | M | T | W | T | F | S |

| S | M | T | W | T | F | S |

| S | M | T | W | T | F | S |

| S | M | T | W | T | F | S |

| S | M | T | W | T | F | S |

PRAYER LIST

_____
_____
_____
_____
_____
_____
_____
_____
_____
_____

APR & MAY	SUNDAY 25	MONDAY 26	TUESDAY 27
PRIORITIES	MORNING	MORNING	MORNING
	DAY	DAY	DAY
	NIGHT	NIGHT	NIGHT

NOTES

WEDNESDAY 28	THURSDAY 29	FRIDAY 30	SATURDAY 1
MORNING	MORNING	MORNING	MORNING
DAY	DAY	DAY	DAY
NIGHT	NIGHT	NIGHT	NIGHT

TO DO LIST

WEEKLY RETREAT • MAY 2, 2021

READING 1	READING 2	GOSPEL
Acts 9:26-31	1 John 3:18-24	John 15:1-8

Remain in me, as I remain in you. Just as a branch cannot bear fruit on its own unless it remains on the vine, so neither can you unless you remain in me. I am the vine, you are the branches. Whoever remains in me and I in him will bear much fruit, because without me you can do nothing.

John 15:4-5

REFLECTION

_____

HOW WERE YOU IN AWE OF GOD THIS WEEK?

WEEKLY RETREAT

FREE SPACE

HABITS & RITUALS

S	M	T	W	T	F	S
S	M	T	W	T	F	S
S	M	T	W	T	F	S
S	M	T	W	T	F	S
S	M	T	W	T	F	S

PRAYER LIST

MAY	SUNDAY 2	MONDAY 3	TUESDAY 4
PRIORITIES	MORNING	MORNING	MORNING
	DAY	DAY	DAY
	NIGHT	NIGHT	NIGHT

NOTES

WEDNESDAY 5	THURSDAY 6	FRIDAY 7	SATURDAY 8
MORNING	MORNING	MORNING	MORNING
DAY	DAY	DAY	DAY
NIGHT	NIGHT	NIGHT	NIGHT

TO DO LIST

WEEKLY RETREAT • MAY 9, 2021

READING 1	READING 2	GOSPEL
Acts 10:25-26, 34-35, 44-48	1 John 4:7-10	John 15:9-17

As the Father loves me, so I also love you. Remain in my love. If you keep my commandments, you will remain in my love, just as I have kept my Father's commandments and remain in his love. I have told you this so that my joy may be in you and your joy may be complete. This is my commandment: love one another as I love you.

John 15:9-12

REFLECTION

HOW WERE YOU IN AWE OF GOD THIS WEEK?

WEEKLY RETREAT

FREE SPACE

HABITS & RITUALS

S	M	T	W	T	F	S
S	M	T	W	T	F	S
S	M	T	W	T	F	S
S	M	T	W	T	F	S
S	M	T	W	T	F	S

PRAYER LIST

MAY	SUNDAY 9	MONDAY 10	TUESDAY 11
PRIORITIES	*Mother's Day*	MORNING	MORNING
	DAY	DAY	DAY
	NIGHT	NIGHT	NIGHT

NOTES

WEDNESDAY 12	THURSDAY 13	FRIDAY 14	SATURDAY 15
MORNING	**The Ascension of the Lord***	MORNING	MORNING
DAY	DAY	DAY	DAY
NIGHT	NIGHT	NIGHT	NIGHT

TO DO LIST

WEEKLY RETREAT • MAY 16, 2021

READING 1	READING 2	GOSPEL
Acts 1:1-11	Ephesians 1:17-23	Mark 16:15-20

These signs will accompany those who believe: in my name they will drive out demons, they will speak new languages. They will pick up serpents [with their hands], and if they drink any deadly thing, it will not harm them. They will lay hands on the sick, and they will recover."

Mark 16:17-18

REFLECTION

HOW WERE YOU IN AWE OF GOD THIS WEEK?

WEEKLY RETREAT

FREE SPACE

HABITS & RITUALS

| S | M | T | W | T | F | S |

| S | M | T | W | T | F | S |

| S | M | T | W | T | F | S |

| S | M | T | W | T | F | S |

| S | M | T | W | T | F | S |

PRAYER LIST

MAY	SUNDAY 16	MONDAY 17	TUESDAY 18
PRIORITIES	The Ascension of the Lord	MORNING	MORNING
	DAY	DAY	DAY
	NIGHT	NIGHT	NIGHT

NOTES

WEDNESDAY 19	THURSDAY 20	FRIDAY 21	SATURDAY 22
MORNING	MORNING	MORNING	MORNING
DAY	DAY	DAY	DAY
NIGHT	NIGHT	NIGHT	NIGHT

TO DO LIST

WEEKLY RETREAT • MAY 23, 2021

READING 1	READING 2	GOSPEL
Genesis 11:1-9	Romans 8:22-27	John 7:37-39

On the last and greatest day of the feast, Jesus stood up and exclaimed, "Let anyone who thirsts come to me and drink.
Whoever believes in me, as scripture says:
'Rivers of living water will flow from within him.'"

John 7:37-38

REFLECTION

HOW WERE YOU IN AWE OF GOD THIS WEEK?

WEEKLY RETREAT

FREE SPACE

HABITS & RITUALS

S	M	T	W	T	F	S
S	M	T	W	T	F	S
S	M	T	W	T	F	S
S	M	T	W	T	F	S
S	M	T	W	T	F	S

PRAYER LIST

MAY	SUNDAY 23	MONDAY 24	TUESDAY 25
PRIORITIES	*Pentecost Sunday*	*Victoria Day (CA)*	MORNING
	DAY	DAY	DAY
	NIGHT	NIGHT	NIGHT

NOTES

WEDNESDAY 26	THURSDAY 27	FRIDAY 28	SATURDAY 29
MORNING	MORNING	MORNING	MORNING
DAY	DAY	DAY	DAY
NIGHT	NIGHT	NIGHT	NIGHT

TO DO LIST

- [ ] _____
- [ ] _____
- [ ] _____
- [ ] _____
- [ ] _____
- [ ] _____
- [ ] _____
- [ ] _____
- [ ] _____
- [ ] _____

- [ ] _____
- [ ] _____
- [ ] _____
- [ ] _____
- [ ] _____
- [ ] _____
- [ ] _____
- [ ] _____
- [ ] _____
- [ ] _____

JUNE	SUNDAY	MONDAY	TUESDAY
NOTES			**1** Saint Justin
	6 The Most Holy Body and Blood of Christ	**7**	**8**
	13 Eleventh Sunday in Ordinary Time	**14** Flag Day	**15**
	20 Twelfth Sunday in Ordinary Time Father's Day	**21** Saint Aloysius Gonzaga	**22** Saint Paulinus of Nola Saints John Fisher & Thomas More
	27 Thirteenth Sunday in Ordinary Time	**28** Saint Irenaeus	**29** Saints Peter & Paul

SAINT JUSTIN

- Feast Day: June 1
- Born: 100; Died: 165
- Patron saint of philosophers
- He was an early Christian apologist, who defended the Christian religion in writing.
- He studied many different schools of philosophy, but was left unsatisfied.
- He encountered an old man who convinced him that the testimony of the prophets were more reliable than the reasoning of philosophers.
- Most of his works are lost, but two apologies and a dialogue did survive.
- He was martyred alongside some of his students.

WEDNESDAY	THURSDAY	FRIDAY	SATURDAY
2 Saints Marcellinus & Peter	3 Saint Charles Lwanga & Companions	4	5 Saint Boniface
9 Saint Ephrem	10	11 The Most Sacred Heart of Jesus Saint Barnabas	12 The Immaculate Heart of the Blessed Virgin Mary
16	17	18	19 Saint Romuald
23	24 The Nativity of Saint John the Baptist	25	26
30 The First Martyrs of the Holy Roman Church			

GOALS

WEEKLY RETREAT • MAY 30, 2021

READING 1	READING 2	GOSPEL
Dt 4:32-34, 39-40	Romans 8:14-17	Matthew 28:16-20

Then Jesus approached and said to them, "All power in heaven and on earth has been given to me. Go, therefore and make disciples of all nations, baptizing them in the name of the Father, and of the Son, and of the holy Spirit, teaching them to observe all that I have commanded you. And behold, I am with you always, until the end of the age."

Matthew 28:18-20

REFLECTION

HOW WERE YOU IN AWE OF GOD THIS WEEK?

WEEKLY RETREAT

FREE SPACE

HABITS & RITUALS

S	M	T	W	T	F	S
S	M	T	W	T	F	S
S	M	T	W	T	F	S
S	M	T	W	T	F	S
S	M	T	W	T	F	S

PRAYER LIST

MAY & JUN	SUNDAY 30	MONDAY 31	TUESDAY 1
PRIORITIES	The Most Holy Trinity	Memorial Day	MORNING
	DAY	DAY	DAY
	NIGHT	NIGHT	NIGHT

NOTES

WEDNESDAY 2	THURSDAY 3	FRIDAY 4	SATURDAY 5
MORNING	MORNING	MORNING	MORNING
DAY	DAY	DAY	DAY
NIGHT	NIGHT	NIGHT	NIGHT

TO DO LIST

WEEKLY RETREAT • JUNE 6, 2021

READING 1	READING 2	GOSPEL
Exodus 24:3-8	Hebrews 9:11-15	Mark 14:12-16, 22-26

He said to them, "This is my blood of the covenant, which will be shed for many. Amen, I say to you, I shall not drink again the fruit of the vine until the day when I drink it new in the kingdom of God."

Mark 14:24-25

REFLECTION

___

HOW WERE YOU IN AWE OF GOD THIS WEEK?

WEEKLY RETREAT

FREE SPACE

HABITS & RITUALS

S	M	T	W	T	F	S
S	M	T	W	T	F	S
S	M	T	W	T	F	S
S	M	T	W	T	F	S
S	M	T	W	T	F	S

PRAYER LIST

JUNE	SUNDAY 6	MONDAY 7	TUESDAY 8
PRIORITIES	The Most Holy Body and Blood of Christ	MORNING	MORNING
	DAY	DAY	DAY
	NIGHT	NIGHT	NIGHT

NOTES

WEDNESDAY 9	THURSDAY 10	FRIDAY 11	SATURDAY 12
MORNING	MORNING	The Most Sacred Heart of Jesus	MORNING
DAY	DAY	DAY	DAY
NIGHT	NIGHT	NIGHT	NIGHT

TO DO LIST

- [ ]
- [ ]
- [ ]
- [ ]
- [ ]
- [ ]
- [ ]
- [ ]
- [ ]
- [ ]

- [ ]
- [ ]
- [ ]
- [ ]
- [ ]
- [ ]
- [ ]
- [ ]
- [ ]
- [ ]

WEEKLY RETREAT • JUNE 13, 2021

READING 1	READING 2	GOSPEL
Exodus 24:3-8	Hebrews 9:11-15	Mark 4:26-34

He said, "This is how it is with the kingdom of God; it is as if a man were to scatter seed on the land and would sleep and rise night and day and the seed would sprout and grow, he knows not how.

Mark 4:26-27

REFLECTION

HOW WERE YOU IN AWE OF GOD THIS WEEK?

WEEKLY RETREAT

FREE SPACE

HABITS & RITUALS

S	M	T	W	T	F	S
S	M	T	W	T	F	S
S	M	T	W	T	F	S
S	M	T	W	T	F	S
S	M	T	W	T	F	S

PRAYER LIST

JUNE	SUNDAY 13	MONDAY 14	TUESDAY 15
PRIORITIES	MORNING	*Flag Day* MORNING	MORNING
	DAY	DAY	DAY
	NIGHT	NIGHT	NIGHT

NOTES

WEDNESDAY 16	THURSDAY 17	FRIDAY 18	SATURDAY 19
MORNING	MORNING	MORNING	MORNING
DAY	DAY	DAY	DAY
NIGHT	NIGHT	NIGHT	NIGHT

TO DO LIST

WEEKLY RETREAT • JUNE 20, 2021

READING 1	READING 2	GOSPEL
Job 38:1, 8-11	2 Corinthians 5:14-17	Mark 4:35-41

Jesus was in the stern, asleep on a cushion. They woke him and said to him, "Teacher, do you not care that we are perishing?" He woke up, rebuked the wind, and said to the sea, "Quiet! Be still!" The wind ceased and there was great calm. Then he asked them, "Why are you terrified? Do you not yet have faith?"

Mark 4:38-40

REFLECTION

HOW WERE YOU IN AWE OF GOD THIS WEEK?

WEEKLY RETREAT

FREE SPACE

HABITS & RITUALS

S	M	T	W	T	F	S
S	M	T	W	T	F	S
S	M	T	W	T	F	S
S	M	T	W	T	F	S
S	M	T	W	T	F	S

PRAYER LIST

JUNE	SUNDAY 20	MONDAY 21	TUESDAY 22
PRIORITIES	*Father's Day*	MORNING	MORNING
	DAY	DAY	DAY
	NIGHT	NIGHT	NIGHT

NOTES

WEDNESDAY 23	THURSDAY 24	FRIDAY 25	SATURDAY 26
MORNING	The Nativity of Saint John the Baptist	MORNING	MORNING
DAY	DAY	DAY	DAY
NIGHT	NIGHT	NIGHT	NIGHT

TO DO LIST

JULY	SUNDAY	MONDAY	TUESDAY
NOTES			
	4 Fourteenth Sunday in Ordinary Time *Independence Day*	**5** Saint Anthony Zaccaria	**6** Saint Maria Goretti
	11 Fifteenth Sunday in Ordinary Time	**12**	**13** Saint Henry
	18 Sixteenth Sunday in Ordinary Time	**19**	**20** Saint Apollinaris
	25 Seventeenth Sunday in Ordinary Time	**26** Saints Joachim & Anne	**27**

SAINT MARIA GORETTI

- Feast Day: July 6
- Born: October 16, 1890; Died: July 6, 1902
- Patron saint of victims of rape, crime victims, teenage girls, and modern youth
- She was born into a farming family.
- When her dad died when she was 9, she took over household duties.

- An 18 year old neighbor tried to make sexual advances and lead her into sin.
- She refused the man and he stabbed her.
- She forgave her murderer before her death two days later.
- The man converted to Christianity in prison after a dream of Maria handing him lilies.

WEDNESDAY	THURSDAY	FRIDAY	SATURDAY
	1 *Canada Day (CA)* Saint Junipero Serra	2	3 Saint Thomas
7	8	9 Saint Augustine Zhao Rong & Companions	10
14 Saint Kateri Tekakwitha	15 Saint Bonaventure	16 Our Lady of Mount Carmel	17
21 Saint Lawrence of Brindisi	22 Saint Mary Magdalene	23 Saint Bridget	24 Saint Sharbel Makhlūf
28	29 Saint Martha	30 Saint Peter Chrysologus	31 Saint Ignatius of Loyola

GOALS

WEEKLY RETREAT • JUNE 27, 2021

READING 1	READING 2	GOSPEL
Wisdom 1:13-15, 2:23-24	2 Corinthians 8:7, 9, 13-15	Mark 5:21-43

One of the synagogue officials, named Jairus, came forward. Seeing him he fell at his feet and pleaded earnestly with him, saying, "My daughter is at the point of death. Please, come lay your hands on her that she may get well and live."

Mark 5:22-23

REFLECTION

HOW WERE YOU IN AWE OF GOD THIS WEEK?

WEEKLY RETREAT

FREE SPACE

HABITS & RITUALS

S	M	T	W	T	F	S
S	M	T	W	T	F	S
S	M	T	W	T	F	S
S	M	T	W	T	F	S
S	M	T	W	T	F	S

PRAYER LIST

JUN & JUL

PRIORITIES

SUNDAY 27
MORNING

DAY

NIGHT

MONDAY 28
MORNING

DAY

NIGHT

TUESDAY 29
Saints Peter and Paul

DAY

NIGHT

NOTES

WEDNESDAY 30	THURSDAY 1	FRIDAY 2	SATURDAY 3
MORNING	*Canada Day (CA)*	MORNING	MORNING
DAY	DAY	DAY	DAY
NIGHT	NIGHT	NIGHT	NIGHT

TO DO LIST

- [ ] _____
- [ ] _____
- [ ] _____
- [ ] _____
- [ ] _____
- [ ] _____
- [ ] _____
- [ ] _____
- [ ] _____
- [ ] _____

- [ ] _____
- [ ] _____
- [ ] _____
- [ ] _____
- [ ] _____
- [ ] _____
- [ ] _____
- [ ] _____
- [ ] _____
- [ ] _____

WEEKLY RETREAT • JULY 4, 2021

READING 1	READING 2	GOSPEL
Ezekiel 2:2-5	2 Corinthians 12:7-10	Mark 6:1-6a

Is he not the carpenter, the son of Mary, and the brother of James and Joses and Judas and Simon? And are not his sisters here with us?" And they took offense at him. Jesus said to them, "A prophet is not without honor except in his native place and among his own kin and in his own house."

Mark 6:3-4

REFLECTION

HOW WERE YOU IN AWE OF GOD THIS WEEK?

WEEKLY RETREAT

FREE SPACE

HABITS & RITUALS

S	M	T	W	T	F	S
S	M	T	W	T	F	S
S	M	T	W	T	F	S
S	M	T	W	T	F	S
S	M	T	W	T	F	S

PRAYER LIST

JULY

PRIORITIES

SUNDAY 4	MONDAY 5	TUESDAY 6
Independence Day		
MORNING	MORNING	MORNING
DAY	DAY	DAY
NIGHT	NIGHT	NIGHT

NOTES

WEDNESDAY 7	THURSDAY 8	FRIDAY 9	SATURDAY 10
MORNING	MORNING	MORNING	MORNING
DAY	DAY	DAY	DAY
NIGHT	NIGHT	NIGHT	NIGHT

TO DO LIST

WEEKLY RETREAT • JULY 11, 2021

READING 1	READING 2	GOSPEL
Amos 7:12-15	Ephesians 1:3-14	Mark 6:7-13

He said to them, "Wherever you enter a house, stay there until you leave from there. Whatever place does not welcome you or listen to you, leave there and shake the dust off your feet in testimony against them." So they went off and preached repentance.

Mark 6:10-12

REFLECTION

HOW WERE YOU IN AWE OF GOD THIS WEEK?

WEEKLY RETREAT

FREE SPACE

HABITS & RITUALS

S	M	T	W	T	F	S
S	M	T	W	T	F	S
S	M	T	W	T	F	S
S	M	T	W	T	F	S
S	M	T	W	T	F	S

PRAYER LIST

JULY	SUNDAY 11	MONDAY 12	TUESDAY 13
PRIORITIES	MORNING	MORNING	MORNING
	DAY	DAY	DAY
	NIGHT	NIGHT	NIGHT

NOTES

WEDNESDAY 14	THURSDAY 15	FRIDAY 16	SATURDAY 17
MORNING	MORNING	MORNING	MORNING
DAY	DAY	DAY	DAY
NIGHT	NIGHT	NIGHT	NIGHT

TO DO LIST

WEEKLY RETREAT • JULY 18, 2021

READING 1	READING 2	GOSPEL
Jeremiah 23:1-6	Ephesians 2:13-18	Mark 6:30-34

When he disembarked and saw the vast crowd, his heart was moved with pity for them, for they were like sheep without a shepherd; and he began to teach them many things.

Mark 6:34

REFLECTION

___

HOW WERE YOU IN AWE OF GOD THIS WEEK?

WEEKLY RETREAT

FREE SPACE

HABITS & RITUALS

S	M	T	W	T	F	S
S	M	T	W	T	F	S
S	M	T	W	T	F	S
S	M	T	W	T	F	S
S	M	T	W	T	F	S

PRAYER LIST

JULY	SUNDAY 18	MONDAY 19	TUESDAY 20
PRIORITIES	MORNING	MORNING	MORNING
	DAY	DAY	DAY
	NIGHT	NIGHT	NIGHT

NOTES

WEDNESDAY 21	THURSDAY 22	FRIDAY 23	SATURDAY 24
MORNING	MORNING	MORNING	MORNING
DAY	DAY	DAY	DAY
NIGHT	NIGHT	NIGHT	NIGHT

TO DO LIST

WEEKLY RETREAT • JULY 25, 2021

READING 1	READING 2	GOSPEL
2 Kings 4:42-44	Ephesians 4:1-6	John 6:1-15

When Jesus raised his eyes and saw that a large crowd was coming to him, he said to Philip, "Where can we buy enough food for them to eat?" He said this to test him, because he himself knew what he was going to do. Philip answered him, "Two hundred days' wages worth of food would not be enough for each of them to have a little [bit]."

John 6:5-7

REFLECTION

HOW WERE YOU IN AWE OF GOD THIS WEEK?

WEEKLY RETREAT

FREE SPACE

HABITS & RITUALS

S	M	T	W	T	F	S
S	M	T	W	T	F	S
S	M	T	W	T	F	S
S	M	T	W	T	F	S
S	M	T	W	T	F	S

PRAYER LIST

JULY	SUNDAY 25	MONDAY 26	TUESDAY 27
PRIORITIES	MORNING	MORNING	MORNING
	DAY	DAY	DAY
	NIGHT	NIGHT	NIGHT

NOTES

WEDNESDAY 28	THURSDAY 29	FRIDAY 30	SATURDAY 31
MORNING	MORNING	MORNING	MORNING
DAY	DAY	DAY	DAY
NIGHT	NIGHT	NIGHT	NIGHT

TO DO LIST

AUGUST	SUNDAY	MONDAY	TUESDAY
NOTES	1 — Eighteenth Sunday in Ordinary Time	2 — *Civic Holiday (CA)* Saint Eusebius of Vercelli Saint Peter Julian Eymard	3
	8 — Ninteenth Sunday in Ordinary Time	9 Saint Teresa Benedicta of the Cross	10 Saint Lawrence
	15 — The Assumption of the Blessed Virgin Mary	16 Saint Stephen of Hungary	17
	22 — Twenty-First Sunday in Ordinary Time	23 Saint Rose of Lima	24 Saint Bartholomew
	29 — Twenty-Second Sunday in Ordinary Time	30	31

SAINT GENESIUS

- Feast Day: August 25
- Died: c. 303
- Patron saint of actors, comedians, and dancers
- He was a leader of a theatrical troupe and performed satirical plays that mocked Christianity.
- He performed in a play mocking baptism with Emperor Diocletian in the audience.
- When he was baptised in the play, he felt a weight on his chest.
- What he felt was the grace of God upon him and he affirmed his new Christian faith in front of the whole audience.
- Diocletian had him arrested, tortured, and later beheaded.

WEDNESDAY	THURSDAY	FRIDAY	SATURDAY
4 Saint John Vianney	5 The Dedication of the Basilica of Saint Mary Major	6 The Transfiguration of the Lord	7 Saint Sixtus II & Companions Saint Cajetan
11 Saint Clare	12 Saint Jane Frances de Chantal	13 Saint Pontian & Hippolytus	14 Saint Maximilian Kolbe
18	19 Saint John Eudes	20 Saint Bernard	21 Saint Pius X
25 Saint Louis Saint Joseph Calasanz	26	27 Saint Monica	28 Saint Augustine

GOALS

WEEKLY RETREAT • AUGUST 1, 2021

READING 1	READING 2	GOSPEL
Exodus 16:2-4, 12-15	Ephesians 4:17, 20-24	John 6:24-35

Do not work for food that perishes but for the food that endures for eternal life, which the Son of Man will give you. For on him the Father, God, has set his seal." So they said to him, "What can we do to accomplish the works of God?" Jesus answered and said to them, "This is the work of God, that you believe in the one he sent."

John 6:27-29

REFLECTION

HOW WERE YOU IN AWE OF GOD THIS WEEK?

WEEKLY RETREAT

FREE SPACE

HABITS & RITUALS

S	M	T	W	T	F	S
S	M	T	W	T	F	S
S	M	T	W	T	F	S
S	M	T	W	T	F	S
S	M	T	W	T	F	S

PRAYER LIST

AUGUST	SUNDAY 1	MONDAY 2	TUESDAY 3
PRIORITIES	MORNING	*Civic Hoiday (CA)*	MORNING
	DAY	DAY	DAY
	NIGHT	NIGHT	NIGHT

NOTES

WEDNESDAY 4	THURSDAY 5	FRIDAY 6	SATURDAY 7
MORNING	MORNING	MORNING	MORNING
DAY	DAY	DAY	DAY
NIGHT	NIGHT	NIGHT	NIGHT

TO DO LIST

- [ ] _____
- [ ] _____
- [ ] _____
- [ ] _____
- [ ] _____
- [ ] _____
- [ ] _____
- [ ] _____
- [ ] _____
- [ ] _____
- [ ] _____

- [ ] _____
- [ ] _____
- [ ] _____
- [ ] _____
- [ ] _____
- [ ] _____
- [ ] _____
- [ ] _____
- [ ] _____
- [ ] _____
- [ ] _____

WEEKLY RETREAT • AUGUST 8, 2021

READING 1	READING 2	GOSPEL
1 Kings 19:4-8	Ephesians 4:30—5:2	John 6:41-51

I am the bread of life. Your ancestors ate the manna in the desert, but they died; this is the bread that comes down from heaven so that one may eat it and not die. I am the living bread that came down from heaven; whoever eats this bread will live forever; and the bread that I will give is my flesh for the life of the world."

John 6:48-51

REFLECTION

HOW WERE YOU IN AWE OF GOD THIS WEEK?

WEEKLY RETREAT

FREE SPACE

HABITS & RITUALS

S	M	T	W	T	F	S
S	M	T	W	T	F	S
S	M	T	W	T	F	S
S	M	T	W	T	F	S
S	M	T	W	T	F	S

PRAYER LIST

AUGUST

PRIORITIES

SUNDAY 8
- MORNING
- DAY
- NIGHT

MONDAY 9
- MORNING
- DAY
- NIGHT

TUESDAY 10
- MORNING
- DAY
- NIGHT

NOTES

WEDNESDAY 11	THURSDAY 12	FRIDAY 13	SATURDAY 14
MORNING	MORNING	MORNING	MORNING
DAY	DAY	DAY	DAY
NIGHT	NIGHT	NIGHT	NIGHT

TO DO LIST

WEEKLY RETREAT • AUGUST 15, 2021

READING 1	READING 2	GOSPEL
1 Chr 15:3-4, 15-16; 16:1-2	1 Corinthians 15:54b-57	Luke 11:27-28

While he was speaking, a woman from the crowd called out and said to him, "Blessed is the womb that carried you and the breasts at which you nursed." He replied, "Rather, blessed are those who hear the word of God and observe it."

Luke 11:27-28

REFLECTION

HOW WERE YOU IN AWE OF GOD THIS WEEK?

WEEKLY RETREAT

FREE SPACE

HABITS & RITUALS

S	M	T	W	T	F	S
S	M	T	W	T	F	S
S	M	T	W	T	F	S
S	M	T	W	T	F	S
S	M	T	W	T	F	S

PRAYER LIST

AUGUST	SUNDAY 15	MONDAY 16	TUESDAY 17
PRIORITIES	**MORNING** The Assumption of the Blessed Virgin Mary	**MORNING**	**MORNING**
	DAY	**DAY**	**DAY**
	NIGHT	**NIGHT**	**NIGHT**

NOTES

WEDNESDAY 18	THURSDAY 19	FRIDAY 20	SATURDAY 21
MORNING	MORNING	MORNING	MORNING
DAY	DAY	DAY	DAY
NIGHT	NIGHT	NIGHT	NIGHT

TO DO LIST

WEEKLY RETREAT • AUGUST 22, 2021

READING 1	READING 2	GOSPEL
Joshua 24:1-2a, 15-17, 18b	Ephesians 5:21-32	John 6:60-69

But there are some of you who do not believe." Jesus knew from the beginning the ones who would not believe and the one who would betray him. And he said, "For this reason I have told you that no one can come to me unless it is granted him by my Father."

John 6:64-65

REFLECTION

___

HOW WERE YOU IN AWE OF GOD THIS WEEK?

WEEKLY RETREAT

FREE SPACE

HABITS & RITUALS

S	M	T	W	T	F	S
S	M	T	W	T	F	S
S	M	T	W	T	F	S
S	M	T	W	T	F	S
S	M	T	W	T	F	S

PRAYER LIST

AUGUST	SUNDAY 22	MONDAY 23	TUESDAY 24
PRIORITIES	MORNING	MORNING	MORNING
	DAY	DAY	DAY
	NIGHT	NIGHT	NIGHT

NOTES

WEDNESDAY 25	THURSDAY 26	FRIDAY 27	SATURDAY 28
MORNING	MORNING	MORNING	MORNING
DAY	DAY	DAY	DAY
NIGHT	NIGHT	NIGHT	NIGHT

TO DO LIST

- [ ] _____
- [ ] _____
- [ ] _____
- [ ] _____
- [ ] _____
- [ ] _____
- [ ] _____
- [ ] _____
- [ ] _____
- [ ] _____

- [ ] _____
- [ ] _____
- [ ] _____
- [ ] _____
- [ ] _____
- [ ] _____
- [ ] _____
- [ ] _____
- [ ] _____
- [ ] _____

SEPTEMBER	SUNDAY	MONDAY	TUESDAY
NOTES			
	5 — Twenty-Third Sunday in Ordinary Time	6 — Labor Day / Labour Day (CA)	7
	12 — Twenty-Fourth Sunday in Ordinary Time	13 — Saint John Chrysostom	14 — The Exaltation of the Holy Cross
	19 — Twenty-Fifth Sunday in Ordinary Time	20 — Saints Andrew Kim Tae-gŏn & Paul Chŏng Ha-sang & Companions	21 — Saint Matthew
	26 — Twenty-Sixth Sunday in Ordinary Time	27 — Saint Vincent de Paul	28 — Saint Wenceslaus / Saint Lawrence Ruiz & Companions

SAINT JOSEPH OF CUPERTINO

- Feast Day: September 18
- Born: June 17, 1603; Died: September 18, 1663
- Patron saint of aviators and astronauts
- Joseph began to experience ecstatic visions as a child, which continued throughout his life.
- His ecstasies made him unfit for duties as a lay brother of the Capuchin friars, so he was dismissed.
- He worked in the stables of the Conventual friars and after several years was admitted to their Order and later ordained a priest.
- His ecstasies began to multiply and he levitated during the Mass for the Divine Office.
- He was deemed disruptive by his superiors and eventually confined to a small cell.

WEDNESDAY	THURSDAY	FRIDAY	SATURDAY
1	2	3 Saint Gregory the Great	4
8 The Nativity of the Blessed Virgin Mary	9 Saint Peter Claver	10	11
15 Our Lady of Sorrows	16 Saints Cornelius & Cyprian	17 Saint Robert Bellarmine	18 Saint Joseph of Cupertino
22	23 Saint Pius of Pietrelcina	24	25
29 Saints Michael, Gabriel, & Raphael	30 Saint Jerome		

GOALS

WEEKLY RETREAT • AUGUST 29, 2021

READING 1	READING 2	GOSPEL
Deuteronomy 4:1-2, 6-8	James 1:17-18, 21b-22, 27	Mark 7:1-8, 14-15, 21-23

He summoned the crowd again and said to them, "Hear me, all of you, and understand. Nothing that enters one from outside can defile that person; but the things that come out from within are what defile."

Mark 7:14-15

REFLECTION

HOW WERE YOU IN AWE OF GOD THIS WEEK?

WEEKLY RETREAT

FREE SPACE

HABITS & RITUALS

S	M	T	W	T	F	S
S	M	T	W	T	F	S
S	M	T	W	T	F	S
S	M	T	W	T	F	S
S	M	T	W	T	F	S

PRAYER LIST

AUG & SEP

PRIORITIES

SUNDAY 29	MONDAY 30	TUESDAY 31
MORNING	MORNING	MORNING
DAY	DAY	DAY
NIGHT	NIGHT	NIGHT

NOTES

WEDNESDAY 1	THURSDAY 2	FRIDAY 3	SATURDAY 4
MORNING	MORNING	MORNING	MORNING
DAY	DAY	DAY	DAY
NIGHT	NIGHT	NIGHT	NIGHT

TO DO LIST

WEEKLY RETREAT • SEPTEMBER 5, 2021

READING 1	READING 2	GOSPEL
Isaiah 35:4-7a	James 2:1-5	Mark 7:31-37

He took him off by himself away from the crowd. He put his finger into the man's ears and, spitting, touched his tongue; then he looked up to heaven and groaned, and said to him, "Ephphatha!" (that is, "Be opened!")

Mark 7:33-34

REFLECTION

___

HOW WERE YOU IN AWE OF GOD THIS WEEK?

WEEKLY RETREAT

FREE SPACE

HABITS & RITUALS

S	M	T	W	T	F	S
S	M	T	W	T	F	S
S	M	T	W	T	F	S
S	M	T	W	T	F	S
S	M	T	W	T	F	S

PRAYER LIST

SEPTEMBER	SUNDAY 5	MONDAY 6	TUESDAY 7
PRIORITIES	MORNING	Labor Day / Labour Day (CA)	MORNING
	DAY	DAY	DAY
	NIGHT	NIGHT	NIGHT

NOTES

WEDNESDAY 8	THURSDAY 9	FRIDAY 10	SATURDAY 11
MORNING	MORNING	MORNING	MORNING
DAY	DAY	DAY	DAY
NIGHT	NIGHT	NIGHT	NIGHT

TO DO LIST

WEEKLY RETREAT • SEPTEMBER 12, 2021

READING 1	READING 2	GOSPEL
Isaiah 50:4c-9a	James 2:14-18	Mark 8:27-35

He spoke this openly. Then Peter took him aside and began to rebuke him. At this he turned around and, looking at his disciples, rebuked Peter and said, "Get behind me, Satan. You are thinking not as God does, but as human beings do."

Mark 8:32-33

REFLECTION

HOW WERE YOU IN AWE OF GOD THIS WEEK?

WEEKLY RETREAT

FREE SPACE

HABITS & RITUALS

S	M	T	W	T	F	S
S	M	T	W	T	F	S
S	M	T	W	T	F	S
S	M	T	W	T	F	S
S	M	T	W	T	F	S

PRAYER LIST

SEPTEMBER	SUNDAY 12	MONDAY 13	TUESDAY 14
PRIORITIES	MORNING	MORNING	MORNING
	DAY	DAY	DAY
	NIGHT	NIGHT	NIGHT

NOTES

WEDNESDAY 15	THURSDAY 16	FRIDAY 17	SATURDAY 18
MORNING	MORNING	MORNING	MORNING
DAY	DAY	DAY	DAY
NIGHT	NIGHT	NIGHT	NIGHT

TO DO LIST

WEEKLY RETREAT • SEPTEMBER 19, 2021

READING 1	READING 2	GOSPEL
Wisdom 2:12, 17-20	James 3:16—4:3	Mark 9:30-37

But they remained silent. They had been discussing among themselves on the way who was the greatest. Then he sat down, called the Twelve, and said to them, "If anyone wishes to be first, he shall be the last of all and the servant of all."

Mark 9:34-35

REFLECTION

HOW WERE YOU IN AWE OF GOD THIS WEEK?

WEEKLY RETREAT

FREE SPACE

HABITS & RITUALS

S	M	T	W	T	F	S
S	M	T	W	T	F	S
S	M	T	W	T	F	S
S	M	T	W	T	F	S
S	M	T	W	T	F	S

PRAYER LIST

SEPTEMBER	SUNDAY 19	MONDAY 20	TUESDAY 21
PRIORITIES	MORNING	MORNING	MORNING
	DAY	DAY	DAY
	NIGHT	NIGHT	NIGHT

NOTES

WEDNESDAY 22	THURSDAY 23	FRIDAY 24	SATURDAY 25
MORNING	MORNING	MORNING	MORNING
DAY	DAY	DAY	DAY
NIGHT	NIGHT	NIGHT	NIGHT

TO DO LIST

- [ ]
- [ ]
- [ ]
- [ ]
- [ ]
- [ ]
- [ ]
- [ ]
- [ ]
- [ ]

- [ ]
- [ ]
- [ ]
- [ ]
- [ ]
- [ ]
- [ ]
- [ ]
- [ ]
- [ ]

OCTOBER	SUNDAY	MONDAY	TUESDAY
NOTES			
	3 Twenty-Seventh Sunday in Ordinary Time	4 *Saint Francis of Assisi*	5 *Blessed Francis Xavier Seelos*
	10 Twenty-Eighth Sunday in Ordinary Time *Saint Francis Borgia*	11 Columbus Day Indigenous Peoples' Day Thanksgiving (CA) *Saint John XXIII*	12
	17 Twenty-Ninth Sunday in Ordinary Time	18 *Saint Luke*	19 *Saints John de Brébeuf & Isaac Jogues & Companions*
	24 Thirtieth Sunday in Ordinary Time	25	26
	31 Thirty-First Sunday in Ordinary Time		

SAINT FRANCIS BORGIA

- Feast Day: October 10
- Born: October 28, 1510; Died: September 30, 1572
- Patron saint of Portugal; against earthquakes
- Francis was the 4th Duke of Gandía.
- When his wife died, he entered the newly formed Society of Jesus.
- He then renounced his titles and became a priest.
- He helped in the establishment of what is now the Gregorian University in Rome.
- He felt drawn to spend time in seclusion and prayer, so he fled to the Basque Country to avoid the Pope's intention to make him a cardinal.
- He later became the Jesuit commissary-general in Spain, where he founded a dozen colleges.

WEDNESDAY	THURSDAY	FRIDAY	SATURDAY
		1 Saint Thérèse of the Child Jesus	2 The Holy Guardian Angels
6 Saint Bruno	7 Our Lady of the Rosary	8	9 Saint Denis Saint John Leonardi
13	14 Saint Callistus I	15 Saint Teresa of Jesus	16 Saint Hedwig Saint Margaret Mary Alacoque
20 Saint Paul of the Cross	21	22 Saint John Paul II	23 Saint John Capistrano
27	28 Saints Simon & Jude	29	30

GOALS

WEEKLY RETREAT • SEPTEMBER 26, 2021

READING 1	READING 2	GOSPEL
Numbers 11:25-29	James 5:1-6	Mark 9:38-43, 45, 47-48

Jesus replied, "Do not prevent him. There is no one who performs a mighty deed in my name who can at the same time speak ill of me. For whoever is not against us is for us. Anyone who gives you a cup of water to drink because you belong to Christ, amen, I say to you, will surely not lose his reward.

Mark 9:39-41

REFLECTION

HOW WERE YOU IN AWE OF GOD THIS WEEK?

WEEKLY RETREAT

FREE SPACE

HABITS & RITUALS

S	M	T	W	T	F	S
S	M	T	W	T	F	S
S	M	T	W	T	F	S
S	M	T	W	T	F	S
S	M	T	W	T	F	S

PRAYER LIST

SEP & OCT	SUNDAY 26	MONDAY 27	TUESDAY 28
PRIORITIES	MORNING	MORNING	MORNING
	DAY	DAY	DAY
	NIGHT	NIGHT	NIGHT

NOTES

WEDNESDAY 29	THURSDAY 30	FRIDAY 1	SATURDAY 2
MORNING	MORNING	MORNING	MORNING
DAY	DAY	DAY	DAY
NIGHT	NIGHT	NIGHT	NIGHT

TO DO LIST

WEEKLY RETREAT • OCTOBER 3, 2021

READING 1	READING 2	GOSPEL
Genesis 2:18-24	Hebrews 2:9-11	Mark 10:2-16

When Jesus saw this he became indignant and said to them, "Let the children come to me; do not prevent them, for the kingdom of God belongs to such as these. Amen, I say to you, whoever does not accept the kingdom of God like a child will not enter it."

Mark 10:14-15

REFLECTION

HOW WERE YOU IN AWE OF GOD THIS WEEK?

WEEKLY RETREAT

FREE SPACE

HABITS & RITUALS

S	M	T	W	T	F	S
S	M	T	W	T	F	S
S	M	T	W	T	F	S
S	M	T	W	T	F	S
S	M	T	W	T	F	S

PRAYER LIST

OCTOBER	SUNDAY 3	MONDAY 4	TUESDAY 5
PRIORITIES	MORNING	MORNING	MORNING
	DAY	DAY	DAY
	NIGHT	NIGHT	NIGHT

NOTES

WEDNESDAY 6	THURSDAY 7	FRIDAY 8	SATURDAY 9
MORNING	MORNING	MORNING	MORNING
DAY	DAY	DAY	DAY
NIGHT	NIGHT	NIGHT	NIGHT

TO DO LIST

- ☐ _____
- ☐ _____
- ☐ _____
- ☐ _____
- ☐ _____
- ☐ _____
- ☐ _____
- ☐ _____
- ☐ _____
- ☐ _____

- ☐ _____
- ☐ _____
- ☐ _____
- ☐ _____
- ☐ _____
- ☐ _____
- ☐ _____
- ☐ _____
- ☐ _____
- ☐ _____

WEEKLY RETREAT • OCTOBER 10, 2021

READING 1	READING 2	GOSPEL
Wisdom 7:7-11	Hebrews 4:12-13	Mark 10:17-30

Jesus, looking at him, loved him and said to him, "You are lacking in one thing. Go, sell what you have, and give to [the] poor and you will have treasure in heaven; then come, follow me." At that statement his face fell, and he went away sad, for he had many possessions.

Mark 10:21-22

REFLECTION

HOW WERE YOU IN AWE OF GOD THIS WEEK?

WEEKLY RETREAT

FREE SPACE

HABITS & RITUALS							PRAYER LIST
S	M	T	W	T	F	S	
S	M	T	W	T	F	S	
S	M	T	W	T	F	S	
S	M	T	W	T	F	S	
S	M	T	W	T	F	S	

OCTOBER

PRIORITIES

SUNDAY 10
- MORNING
- DAY
- NIGHT

MONDAY 11
Columbus Day
Indigenous Peoples' Day
Thanksgiving (CA)

- DAY
- NIGHT

TUESDAY 12
- MORNING
- DAY
- NIGHT

NOTES

WEDNESDAY 13	THURSDAY 14	FRIDAY 15	SATURDAY 16
MORNING	MORNING	MORNING	MORNING
DAY	DAY	DAY	DAY
NIGHT	NIGHT	NIGHT	NIGHT

TO DO LIST

WEEKLY RETREAT • OCTOBER 17, 2021

READING 1	READING 2	GOSPEL
Isaiah 53:10-11	Hebrews 4:14-16	Mark 10:35-45

But it shall not be so among you. Rather, whoever wishes to be great among you will be your servant; whoever wishes to be first among you will be the slave of all. For the Son of Man did not come to be served but to serve and to give his life as a ransom for many."

Mark 10:43-45

REFLECTION

HOW WERE YOU IN AWE OF GOD THIS WEEK?

WEEKLY RETREAT

FREE SPACE

HABITS & RITUALS

S	M	T	W	T	F	S
S	M	T	W	T	F	S
S	M	T	W	T	F	S
S	M	T	W	T	F	S
S	M	T	W	T	F	S

PRAYER LIST

OCTOBER	SUNDAY 17	MONDAY 18	TUESDAY 19
PRIORITIES	MORNING	MORNING	MORNING
	DAY	DAY	DAY
	NIGHT	NIGHT	NIGHT

NOTES

WEDNESDAY 20	THURSDAY 21	FRIDAY 22	SATURDAY 23
MORNING	MORNING	MORNING	MORNING
DAY	DAY	DAY	DAY
NIGHT	NIGHT	NIGHT	NIGHT

TO DO LIST

WEEKLY RETREAT • OCTOBER 24, 2021

READING 1	READING 2	GOSPEL
Jeremiah 31:7-9	Hebrews 5:1-6	Mark 10:46-52

Jesus said to him in reply, "What do you want me to do for you?" The blind man replied to him, "Master, I want to see." Jesus told him, "Go your way; your faith has saved you." Immediately he received his sight and followed him on the way.

Mark 10:51-52

REFLECTION

_____

HOW WERE YOU IN AWE OF GOD THIS WEEK?

WEEKLY RETREAT

FREE SPACE

HABITS & RITUALS

| S | M | T | W | T | F | S |

| S | M | T | W | T | F | S |

| S | M | T | W | T | F | S |

| S | M | T | W | T | F | S |

| S | M | T | W | T | F | S |

PRAYER LIST

OCTOBER	SUNDAY 24	MONDAY 25	TUESDAY 26
PRIORITIES	MORNING	MORNING	MORNING
	DAY	DAY	DAY
	NIGHT	NIGHT	NIGHT

NOTES

WEDNESDAY 27	THURSDAY 28	FRIDAY 29	SATURDAY 30
MORNING	MORNING	MORNING	MORNING
DAY	DAY	DAY	DAY
NIGHT	NIGHT	NIGHT	NIGHT

TO DO LIST

NOVEMBER

NOTES

SUNDAY	MONDAY	TUESDAY
	1 All Saints	**2** All Souls' Day
7 Thirty-Second Sunday in Ordinary Time — *Daylight Saving Time End*	**8**	**9** The Dedication of the Lateran Basilica
14 Thirty-Third Sunday in Ordinary Time	**15** Saint Albert the Great	**16** Saint Margaret of Scotland / Saint Gertrude
21 Our Lord Jesus Christ, King of the Universe	**22** Saint Cecilia	**23** Saint Clement I / Saint Columban / Blessed Miguel Agustin Pro
28 First Sunday of Advent	**29**	**30** Saint Andrew

SAINT CATHERINE OF ALEXANDRIA

- Feast Day: November 25
- Born: c. 287; Died: c. 305
- Patron saint of unmarried girls, educators, nurses, librarians, and craftsmen who work with a wheel
- Emperor Maxentius summoned 50 pagan philosophers to debate with Catherine.
- Several philosophers converted after her win.
- Catherine was imprisoned and had many visitors, including Maxentius' wife, who converted.
- When she was released, a bright light and fragrant perfume filled the dungeon.
- She refused the emperor's marriage proposal.
- She was condemned to death on a spiked breaking wheel, but it shattered at her touch.

WEDNESDAY	THURSDAY	FRIDAY	SATURDAY
3 Saint Martin de Porres	4 Saint Charles Borromeo	5	6
10 Saint Leo the Great	11 *Veterans Day* *Remembrance Day (CA)* Saint Martin of Tours	12 Saint Josaphat	13 Saint Francis Xavier Cabrini
17 Saint Elizabeth of Hungary	18 The Dedication of the Basilicas of Saints Peter & Paul Saint Rose Philippine Duschesne	19	20
24 Saint Andrew Dũng-Lạc	25 *Thanksgiving* Saint Catherine of Alexandria	26	27

GOALS

WEEKLY RETREAT • OCTOBER 31, 2021

READING 1	READING 2	GOSPEL
Deuteronomy 6:2-6	Hebrews 7:23-28	Mark 12:28b-34

The scribe said to him, "Well said, teacher. You are right in saying, 'He is One and there is no other than he.' And 'to love him with all your heart, with all your understanding, with all your strength, and to love your neighbor as yourself' is worth more than all burnt offerings and sacrifices."

Mark 12:32-33

REFLECTION

HOW WERE YOU IN AWE OF GOD THIS WEEK?

WEEKLY RETREAT

FREE SPACE

HABITS & RITUALS

S	M	T	W	T	F	S
S	M	T	W	T	F	S
S	M	T	W	T	F	S
S	M	T	W	T	F	S
S	M	T	W	T	F	S

PRAYER LIST

OCT & NOV	SUNDAY 31	MONDAY 1	TUESDAY 2
PRIORITIES	MORNING	All Saints	All Souls' Day
	DAY	DAY	DAY
	NIGHT	NIGHT	NIGHT

NOTES

WEDNESDAY 3	THURSDAY 4	FRIDAY 5	SATURDAY 6
MORNING	MORNING	MORNING	MORNING
DAY	DAY	DAY	DAY
NIGHT	NIGHT	NIGHT	NIGHT

TO DO LIST

- ☐ _____
- ☐ _____
- ☐ _____
- ☐ _____
- ☐ _____
- ☐ _____
- ☐ _____
- ☐ _____
- ☐ _____
- ☐ _____

- ☐ _____
- ☐ _____
- ☐ _____
- ☐ _____
- ☐ _____
- ☐ _____
- ☐ _____
- ☐ _____
- ☐ _____
- ☐ _____

WEEKLY RETREAT • NOVEMBER 7, 2021

READING 1	READING 2	GOSPEL
1 Kings 17:10-16	Hebrews 9:24-28	Mark 12:38-44

In the course of his teaching he said, "Beware of the scribes, who like to go around in long robes and accept greetings in the marketplaces, seats of honor in synagogues, and places of honor at banquets.

Mark 12:38-39

REFLECTION

HOW WERE YOU IN AWE OF GOD THIS WEEK?

WEEKLY RETREAT

FREE SPACE

HABITS & RITUALS

| S | M | T | W | T | F | S |

| S | M | T | W | T | F | S |

| S | M | T | W | T | F | S |

| S | M | T | W | T | F | S |

| S | M | T | W | T | F | S |

PRAYER LIST

NOVEMBER	SUNDAY 7	MONDAY 8	TUESDAY 9
PRIORITIES	*Daylight Saving Time End* MORNING	MORNING	MORNING
	DAY	DAY	DAY
	NIGHT	NIGHT	NIGHT

NOTES

WEDNESDAY 10	THURSDAY 11	FRIDAY 12	SATURDAY 13
MORNING	*Veterans Day* *Remembrance Day (CA)*	MORNING	MORNING
DAY	DAY	DAY	DAY
NIGHT	NIGHT	NIGHT	NIGHT

TO DO LIST

- [ ]
- [ ]
- [ ]
- [ ]
- [ ]
- [ ]
- [ ]
- [ ]
- [ ]
- [ ]

- [ ]
- [ ]
- [ ]
- [ ]
- [ ]
- [ ]
- [ ]
- [ ]
- [ ]
- [ ]

WEEKLY RETREAT • NOVEMBER 14, 2021

READING 1	READING 2	GOSPEL
Daniel 12:1-3	Hebrews 10:11-14, 18	Mark 13:24-32

"Learn a lesson from the fig tree. When its branch becomes tender and sprouts leaves, you know that summer is near. In the same way, when you see these things happening, know that he is near, at the gates.

Mark 13:28-29

REFLECTION

HOW WERE YOU IN AWE OF GOD THIS WEEK?

WEEKLY RETREAT

FREE SPACE

HABITS & RITUALS	PRAYER LIST

S	M	T	W	T	F	S
S	M	T	W	T	F	S
S	M	T	W	T	F	S
S	M	T	W	T	F	S
S	M	T	W	T	F	S

NOVEMBER	SUNDAY 14	MONDAY 15	TUESDAY 16
PRIORITIES	MORNING	MORNING	MORNING
	DAY	DAY	DAY
	NIGHT	NIGHT	NIGHT

NOTES

WEDNESDAY 17	THURSDAY 18	FRIDAY 19	SATURDAY 20
MORNING	MORNING	MORNING	MORNING
DAY	DAY	DAY	DAY
NIGHT	NIGHT	NIGHT	NIGHT

TO DO LIST

WEEKLY RETREAT • NOVEMBER 21, 2021

READING 1	READING 2	GOSPEL
Daniel 7:13-14	Revelation 1:5-8	John 18:33b-37

So Pilate said to him, "Then you are a king?" Jesus answered, "You say I am a king. For this I was born and for this I came into the world, to testify to the truth. Everyone who belongs to the truth listens to my voice."

John 18:37

REFLECTION

HOW WERE YOU IN AWE OF GOD THIS WEEK?

WEEKLY RETREAT

FREE SPACE

HABITS & RITUALS

S	M	T	W	T	F	S
S	M	T	W	T	F	S
S	M	T	W	T	F	S
S	M	T	W	T	F	S
S	M	T	W	T	F	S

PRAYER LIST

NOVEMBER	SUNDAY 21	MONDAY 22	TUESDAY 23
PRIORITIES	Our Lord Jesus Christ, King of the Universe	MORNING	MORNING
	DAY	DAY	DAY
	NIGHT	NIGHT	NIGHT

NOTES

WEDNESDAY 24	THURSDAY 25	FRIDAY 26	SATURDAY 27
MORNING	*Thanksgiving*	MORNING	MORNING
DAY	DAY	DAY	DAY
NIGHT	NIGHT	NIGHT	NIGHT

TO DO LIST

- [ ] _____
- [ ] _____
- [ ] _____
- [ ] _____
- [ ] _____
- [ ] _____
- [ ] _____
- [ ] _____
- [ ] _____
- [ ] _____

- [ ] _____
- [ ] _____
- [ ] _____
- [ ] _____
- [ ] _____
- [ ] _____
- [ ] _____
- [ ] _____
- [ ] _____
- [ ] _____

DECEMBER	SUNDAY	MONDAY	TUESDAY
NOTES			
	5 Second Sunday of Advent	6 Saint Nicholas	7 Saint Ambrose
	12 Third Sunday of Advent	13 Saint Lucy	14 Saint John of the Cross
	19 Fourth Sunday of Advent	20	21 Saint Peter Canisius
	26 The Holy Family of Jesus, Mary and Joseph *Boxing Day (CA)*	27 Saint John	28 The Holy Innocents

SAINT FRANCIS XAVIER

- Feast Day: December 3
- Born: April 7, 1506; Died: December 2, 1552
- Patron saint of missionaries and missions
- Saint Ignatius convinced Francis to become a priest while both attended the University of Paris.
- Francis, Ignatius, and other friends vowed to travel to the Holy Land to convert non-believers.
- Francis was appointed by Ignatius to help establish the Society of Jesus (the Jesuits) in Portugal. Thus, beginning his life as the first Jesuit missionary.
- Francis devoted much of his life to missions especially in Asia - mainly Malacca, Amboina and Ternate, Japan, and off-shore China.

WEDNESDAY	THURSDAY	FRIDAY	SATURDAY
1	2	3 Saint Francis Xavier	4 Saint John Damascene
8 The Immaculate Conception of the Blessed Virgin Mary	9 Saint Juan Diego	10 Our Lady of Loreto	11 Saint Damasus I
15	16	17	18
22	23 Saint John of Kanty	24	25 The Nativity of the Lord, Christmas
29 Saint Thomas Becket	30	31 Saint Sylvester I	

GOALS

WEEKLY RETREAT • NOVEMBER 28, 2021

READING 1	READING 2	GOSPEL
Jeremiah 33:14-16	1 Thessalonians 3:12—4:2	Luke 21:25-28, 34-36

"Beware that your hearts do not become drowsy from carousing and drunkenness and the anxieties of daily life, and that day catch you by surprise like a trap. For that day will assault everyone who lives on the face of the earth.

Luke 21:34-35

REFLECTION

HOW WERE YOU IN AWE OF GOD THIS WEEK?

WEEKLY RETREAT

FREE SPACE

HABITS & RITUALS	PRAYER LIST
S M T W T F S	
S M T W T F S	
S M T W T F S	
S M T W T F S	
S M T W T F S	

NOV & DEC	SUNDAY 28	MONDAY 29	TUESDAY 30
PRIORITIES	MORNING	MORNING	MORNING
	DAY	DAY	DAY
	NIGHT	NIGHT	NIGHT

NOTES

WEDNESDAY	THURSDAY	FRIDAY	SATURDAY
1	**2**	**3**	**4**
MORNING	MORNING	MORNING	MORNING
DAY	DAY	DAY	DAY
NIGHT	NIGHT	NIGHT	NIGHT

TO DO LIST

- ☐ _____
- ☐ _____
- ☐ _____
- ☐ _____
- ☐ _____
- ☐ _____
- ☐ _____
- ☐ _____
- ☐ _____
- ☐ _____

- ☐ _____
- ☐ _____
- ☐ _____
- ☐ _____
- ☐ _____
- ☐ _____
- ☐ _____
- ☐ _____
- ☐ _____
- ☐ _____

WEEKLY RETREAT • DECEMBER 5, 2021

READING 1	READING 2	GOSPEL
Baruch 5:1-9	Philippians 1:5-6, 8-11	Luke 3:1-6

Every valley shall be filled and every mountain and hill shall be made low. The winding roads shall be made straight, and the rough ways made smooth, and all flesh shall see the salvation of God.'"

Luke 3:5-6

REFLECTION

HOW WERE YOU IN AWE OF GOD THIS WEEK?

WEEKLY RETREAT

FREE SPACE

HABITS & RITUALS

S	M	T	W	T	F	S
S	M	T	W	T	F	S
S	M	T	W	T	F	S
S	M	T	W	T	F	S
S	M	T	W	T	F	S

PRAYER LIST

| DECEMBER | SUNDAY 5 | MONDAY 6 | TUESDAY 7 |

PRIORITIES

MORNING	MORNING	MORNING
DAY	DAY	DAY
NIGHT	NIGHT	NIGHT

NOTES

WEDNESDAY 8	THURSDAY 9	FRIDAY 10	SATURDAY 11
The Immaculate Conception of the Blessed Virgin Mary	MORNING	MORNING	MORNING
DAY	DAY	DAY	DAY
NIGHT	NIGHT	NIGHT	NIGHT

TO DO LIST

- [ ] _____
- [ ] _____
- [ ] _____
- [ ] _____
- [ ] _____
- [ ] _____
- [ ] _____
- [ ] _____
- [ ] _____
- [ ] _____

- [ ] _____
- [ ] _____
- [ ] _____
- [ ] _____
- [ ] _____
- [ ] _____
- [ ] _____
- [ ] _____
- [ ] _____
- [ ] _____

WEEKLY RETREAT • DECEMBER 12, 2021

READING 1	READING 2	GOSPEL
Zephaniah 3:14-18a	Philippians 4:4-7	Luke 3:10-18

John answered them all, saying, "I am baptizing you with water, but one mightier than I is coming. I am not worthy to loosen the thongs of his sandals. He will baptize you with the holy Spirit and fire.

Luke 3:16

REFLECTION

HOW WERE YOU IN AWE OF GOD THIS WEEK?

WEEKLY RETREAT

FREE SPACE

HABITS & RITUALS

| S | M | T | W | T | F | S |

| S | M | T | W | T | F | S |

| S | M | T | W | T | F | S |

| S | M | T | W | T | F | S |

| S | M | T | W | T | F | S |

PRAYER LIST

DECEMBER	SUNDAY 12	MONDAY 13	TUESDAY 14
PRIORITIES	MORNING	MORNING	MORNING
	DAY	DAY	DAY
	NIGHT	NIGHT	NIGHT

NOTES

WEDNESDAY 15	THURSDAY 16	FRIDAY 17	SATURDAY 18
MORNING	MORNING	MORNING	MORNING
DAY	DAY	DAY	DAY
NIGHT	NIGHT	NIGHT	NIGHT

TO DO LIST

WEEKLY RETREAT • DECEMBER 19, 2021

READING 1	READING 2	GOSPEL
Micah 5:1-4a	Hebrews 10:5-10	Luke 1:39-45

When Elizabeth heard Mary's greeting, the infant leaped in her womb, and Elizabeth, filled with the holy Spirit, cried out in a loud voice and said, "Most blessed are you among women, and blessed is the fruit of your womb.

Luke 1:41-42

REFLECTION

_____
_____
_____
_____
_____
_____
_____
_____
_____
_____
_____
_____
_____
_____
_____
_____
_____
_____

HOW WERE YOU IN AWE OF GOD THIS WEEK?

WEEKLY RETREAT

FREE SPACE

HABITS & RITUALS

S	M	T	W	T	F	S
S	M	T	W	T	F	S
S	M	T	W	T	F	S
S	M	T	W	T	F	S
S	M	T	W	T	F	S

PRAYER LIST

DECEMBER	SUNDAY 19	MONDAY 20	TUESDAY 21
PRIORITIES	MORNING	MORNING	MORNING
	DAY	DAY	DAY
	NIGHT	NIGHT	NIGHT

NOTES

WEDNESDAY 22	THURSDAY 23	FRIDAY 24	SATURDAY 25
MORNING	MORNING	MORNING	**The Nativity of the Lord Christmas**
DAY	DAY	DAY	DAY
NIGHT	NIGHT	NIGHT	NIGHT

TO DO LIST

WEEKLY RETREAT • DECEMBER 26, 2021

READING 1	READING 2	GOSPEL
Sirach 3:2-6, 12-14	Colossians 3:12-21	Luke 2:41-52

When his parents saw him, they were astonished, and his mother said to him, "Son, why have you done this to us? Your father and I have been looking for you with great anxiety." And he said to them, "Why were you looking for me? Did you not know that I must be in my Father's house?"

Luke 2:48-49

REFLECTION

_____
_____
_____
_____
_____
_____
_____
_____
_____
_____
_____
_____
_____
_____
_____
_____
_____

HOW WERE YOU IN AWE OF GOD THIS WEEK?

WEEKLY RETREAT

FREE SPACE

HABITS & RITUALS

| S | M | T | W | T | F | S |

| S | M | T | W | T | F | S |

| S | M | T | W | T | F | S |

| S | M | T | W | T | F | S |

| S | M | T | W | T | F | S |

PRAYER LIST

DEC & JAN

PRIORITIES

SUNDAY 26
Boxing Day (CA)

DAY

NIGHT

MONDAY 27
MORNING

DAY

NIGHT

TUESDAY 28
MORNING

DAY

NIGHT

NOTES

WEDNESDAY 29	THURSDAY 30	FRIDAY 31	SATURDAY 1
MORNING	MORNING	MORNING	*New Year's Day*
DAY	DAY	DAY	DAY
NIGHT	NIGHT	NIGHT	NIGHT

TO DO LIST

YEAR END REVIEW

Congratulations! You made it through 2021!
Look back at your Path to Sainthood and reflect on the year you accomplished.

Scripture texts in this work are taken from the *New American Bible, revised edition* © 2010, 1991, 1986, 1970 Confraternity of Christian Doctrine, Washington, D.C. and are used by permission of the copyright owner. All Rights Reserved. No part of the New American Bible may be reproduced in any form without permission in writing from the copyright owner.